Animal EYES

Cataloging Information

Fielding, Beth.
    Animal eyes/Beth Fielding
        36 p. : col. ill. ; 20 cm.
    Includes index (p.).
    Summary: Explores the morphology and behavior of animal eyes.
        Includes a range of taxa, including mammals, insects,
        birds, reptiles, amphibians, and mollusks.
    LC: QL 946
    Dewey: 591.4
    ISBN-13: 978-0-9797455-5-3 (alk. paper)
    ISBN-10:   0-9797455-5-1 (alk. paper)
        Eye —Juvenile literature

Cover Design: Cindy LaBreacht
Art Director: Susan McBride
Editor: Catherine Ham
Editorial Assistance: Katy Nelson
Copy Editor: Susan Brill
Photo Research: Dawn Cusick

To the world's science teachers
who work so hard to help us see

10 9 8 7 6 5 4 3 2 1

First edition

Published by EarlyLight Books, Inc.
1436 Dellwood Road
Waynesville, NC 28786

ISBN 13: 978-0-9797455-5-3

ISBN 10:0-9797455-5-1

Dragonfly nymph

Animal EYES

BETH FIELDING

EarlyLight Books

WAYNESVILLE, NORTH CAROLINA, USA

BULGING EYES

HIDING EYES

STRIPED EYES

STARING EYES

BALLOON EYES

HIDING EYES

GLOW-IN-THE-DARK EYES

SEE-IN-THE-DARK EYES

TRICK EYES

FANCY EYES

FAKE EYES

SHEDDING EYES

DRAGON EYES

WINKING EYES

BLINKING EYES

PRIZE EYES

CURIOUS EYES

TEST IT OUT: Can you see color at night as well as you can during the day? To find out, spread out a large box of crayons or colored pencils on a table in the morning. Carefully study the colors in front of you. How many shades of yellow do you see? How many shades of blue? Of red? Later in the day, as the sun starts going down, look at the crayons or pencils again. Do you still see the same colors? When it's almost dark outside, look at the crayons again. How many colors do you see now?

PEOPLE EYES

Babies are born with very large eyes. Look at your eyes in a mirror. If you are older than six, your eyes have almost finished growing! Human eyes are amazing. We see more colors than most animals, although some some insects, birds, and shrimp see more colors than we do.

People can also do some really cool tricks with their eyes that many animals cannot do. Without moving your head, look as far as you can to your left, then to your right, then up, then down. When a bird wants to look left or right, or up or down, they have to move their entire head. If an insect wants to look left or right, or up or down, it has to move its entire body!

HOW OUR EYES WORK . . . Our eyes have several parts to them, and each part does something important. The pupil is the black circle in the middle of your eye and is the place where light enters the eye. Did you do the **Test It Out** experiment on the left-hand page? When your eyes sensed less light, muscles in your eye opened your pupils wider to let more light into your eye. A human pupil is usually about 2 mm wide in bright sunlight and 8 mm wide in the dark! To learn more about our eyes and how they work, see page 36.

CAT EYES

A house cat may look very different from a lion or a tiger, but its eyes work the same way. Because most wild cats are night hunters, they need very good night vision. At night and in low light, a cat's pupils get big and round, which lets in more light.

In bright sunlight, cat pupils are shaped like tall slits. This type of pupil shape is called eliptical, and is found in many animals that are active during both the day and the night. The slit shape works like sunglasses, blocking bright light from damaging the cat's eyes.

Cats do not see colors the same way we do. Like dogs, they can see black, white, gray, and blue. Shades of green and red look almost the same to them. Here's a shopping tip: Never buy an outdoor toy for a dog that's red or dark orange — he or she will have trouble finding it in green grass!

GLOW-IN-THE-DARK EYES?
Cat eyes do not really glow in the dark, but they can look like they are glowing if someone shines a light on them at night. Why? Cats have a mirror-like tissue layer, called a tapetum, at the back of each eye, which reflects light.

TEST IT OUT: Go into a room tonight after the sun goes down and shut the door. Turn out the lights. At first you can't see well, right? After a few minutes, your pupils get larger, allowing some of the light from under the door into your eyes, helping you to see better. If you were a cat, though, your pupils would have changed size in seconds, not minutes!

ELEPHANT EYES

Elephants are the largest animals that live on land, but they do not have the largest eyes. In fact, they have very tiny eyes and do not see well. Elephant eyes are on the sides of their heads, so to see in front of their bodies, they have to move their heads back and forth. Elephants do have good hearing and a strong sense of smell.

Elephants have three eyelids with super-long eyelashes to help keep dust and mud out of their eyes. The extra eyelids also protect their eyes when they are pulling down tree branches with their trunks and lifting them to their mouths to eat.

GUESS WHAT? Just like many other animals, elephants wink! Scientists think elephants wink to clean dirt out of their eyes, or to move bugs away from their eyes, or maybe just because . . .

Some animals, such as the dog shown here, can be trained to wink!

MORE COOL EYES: The tarsier (left) from Southeast Asia has the largest eyes for its body size of any animal.

Lemurs and raccoons (right) wear a "mask" of dark fur around their eyes. Some biologists think the mask makes their stare look scarier to their enemies.

LEMUR EYES

The word lemur comes from the Spanish word for ghost. Lemurs may have been named after ghosts because they sleep in trees and their eyes shine at night. Or maybe because the black fur around their eyes looks like a scary mask. Or maybe because lemurs make ghost-like sounds when they talk to each other.

There are more than 33 types (species) of lemurs. They all live in Madagascar, an island off the coast of Africa. Most lemurs have orange or yellow eyes, but a few have blue eyes. Like birds, lemurs cannot move their eyes the way we can, so they have to turn their heads to see something that is not right in front of them.

The animal below is a ring-tailed lemur. It is about the size of a house cat and is active during the day, eating berries, leaves, and insects. Do you see how small its pupils are? The animal on the left-hand page is a mouse lemur. Like most nocturnal lemurs, the mouse lemur has a small body and very large eyes with extra-wide pupils.

BIRD EYES

Birds use their eyes to find food, so good eyesight is very important for them. The pupils in bird eyes are round and very large, while the iris — the colored area around the pupil — is very small. You almost never see the white area of a bird's eye because their pupils are so large.

Although many types of animals do not see in color, birds see color much better than people do. Birds see more colors than we do, plus the colors they see are brighter than the colors we see.

Birds have a clear eyelid called a nictitating membrane. Sharks, reptiles, and amphibians do, too. When they blink, the membrane in each eye dampens and cleans the eye, the same way our upper eyelids work when we blink.

TEST IT OUT: Watch the birds in your neighborhood or a zoo for at least 15 minutes. How often do they move their heads? Since they do not have muscles to move just their eyes, birds move their heads from side to side a lot so they can see food and predators around them.

WHAT'S FOR DINNER? Birds such as the owl (left) that hunt other animals for food usually have eyes on the front of their heads, the way people do. Birds that eat seeds, such as the toucan (top left) and parrots (middle left and right-hand page, top) usually have eyes on the sides of their heads.

The ostrich takes the prize for the largest eyes of any land animal, more than 5 cm wide!

Ostriches cannot see as far as owls, but their long necks help them move closer to things they want to see.

CHAMELEON
EYES

You may have heard about the chameleon's amazing tongue. The tongue has a sticky tip that shoots out of the chameleon's mouth super fast, letting it catch flying insects. An amazing tongue would not do a chameleon any good, though, if it didn't have great vision to see the fast-moving insects it wants to catch.

A chameleon can do a special trick with its eyes. It can move its left eye in one direction and its right eye in another direction. This trick lets chameleons see bugs — and predators — in all directions at the same time!

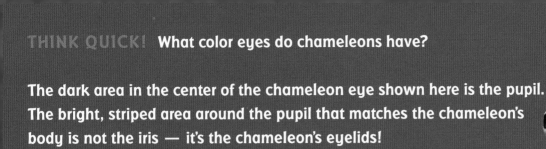

The dark area in the center of the chameleon eye shown here is the pupil. The bright, striped area around the pupil that matches the chameleon's body is not the iris — it's the chameleon's eyelids!

The eyelids are fused together around the pupil, and these fused eyelids work like sunglasses to protect the chameleon's eyes when it hunts in bright sun during the day.

MORE FANCY EYES: The eyelids of this water dragon (right), green tree lizard (below left), and bearded dragon (below right) also have patterns that match their bodies.

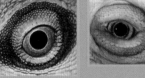

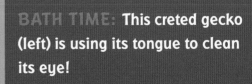

TOTALLY COOL: Pit vipers have special places called pits between their eyes. The pits allow them to sense changes in air temperature caused by other animals, especially by favorite prey such as warm-blooded mice and rats.

SNAKE EYES

Say this line three times, very fast: Snake stares scare silly people. Snake stares scare silly people. Snake stares scare silly people. Why are some people so scared when a snake stares at them? Snakes do not have blinking eyelids, the way people do, so even though it looks like they are looking straight at you, they are not. In fact, most snakes do not see very well and find their prey with their sense of smell.

You may read that venomous snakes have eliptical pupils, shaped like a cat's pupils in bright light, and that nonvenomous snakes have round pupils. This is not always true, though; only a snake expert can tell if the bite from a certain snake will hurt you.

When snakes are about to shed their skin, also known as molting, their eyes may take on a bluish, cloudy haze. The cloudy haze on their eyes disappears after the old skin sheds.

GOOD NEWS, BAD NEWS: Turtles
have very good eyesight when their eyes
are under water. Above the water, though, they can only see things
that are close to them.

ALLIGATOR EYES

The next time you are at the beach or in a swimming pool, try this experiment. Place your face in the water and use your arms and legs to swim forward. Even if you are wearing a diving mask or swimming goggles, you probably cannot see the ground very clearly. Can you see the land while your face is in the water?

Alligators, crocodiles, and caimans have eyes high on top of their heads, which let them see above the water while their bodies hide under the water. To find out where crocodile eyes are, look down at the ground and find your ears with your hands — that's about where your eyes would be if you were a crocodile.

When you brush your teeth tonight, look in the mirror at your eyelids. You have two eyelids for each eye — a large eyelid on top and a smaller one on the bottom. Alligators, crocodiles, and caimans have THREE eyelids! Their third eyelid is a clear membrane — called a nictitating membrane — that works like built-in swimming goggles to protect their eyes while they dive under water. Birds, sharks, and amphibians also have nictitating membranes.

FROG EYES

To learn the coolest thing about frog eyes, you will need a big bite of cake. Or a big bite of pizza. Or a big bite of your favorite fruit. Chew the food well and then swallow it. That was easy, right? Your tongue helps move the food to the back of your mouth and then special muscles in your throat move the food down to your stomach.

When a frog eats a yummy bug or fish, the frog does not use its tongue to move the food to the back of its throat. Instead, a frog uses its eyes to help move the food down its throat. No kidding! The frog's eyes move down into its skull and push the food down to its stomach.

If you watch a frog eat, you won't see its eyeballs move, though. Frogs have two eyelids for each eye — an inner eyelid and an outer eyelid. When the frog's eyeballs move down into its skull, it pulls the two eyelids together so they tightly close. Frogs can also close both eyelids when they go under water, which protects their eyes from being scratched by sticks or rocks.

TEST IT OUT: Pretend you are a frog the next time you eat with friends or family. Quickly close and re-open your eyes every time you swallow a bite of food. How long does it take someone to ask why you are acting so silly?

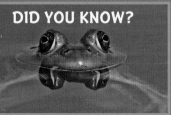
Frog eyes are found on the sides of their heads when they are tadpoles and on top of their heads when they are adults.

Frog eyes are like balloons, bulging outward, which lets them see more of the area around them.

Frog eyes come in lots of colors, from red to gold to green, and often match their bodies.

FISH EYES

Fish eyes are like people eyes in some ways. Fish have a pupil in the center of each eye. They also they have six eye muscles, just like we do, so they can move their eyes without moving their heads. Most fish have very good vision and can see colors. Fish do not have eyelids like we do, though, so they can'not blink their upper and lower eyelids together the way we do to clean our eyes.

Many types of fish are named after their eyes. Some types of pet fish, such as the goldfish, are bred for their unusual eyes. The dragon eye goldfish has large, protruding eyes (above right). The bubble eye goldfish (above left and at right), has large, balloon-like sacs of air that bulge out.

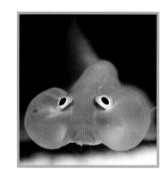

The short-nose greeneye fish (right-hand page) has glow-in-the-dark eyes! It lives near the bottom of deep oceans and may use the light from its glowing eyes to help it find food.

NOT GUILTY! Some people think that sharks have black eyes, but that's not true. When a shark's pupils are fully dilated, it might look like they have black eyes because the pupil is so large it fills the eye area.

Just like cats, sharks have a tapetum, a mirror-like area in the back of their eyes that lets them use more light. Many types of sharks have very good eyesight.

RIGHT-HAND PAGE, BOTTOM: Fish eyes have amazing colors and patterns. Some fish eyes even have stripes that help the fish hide from predators.

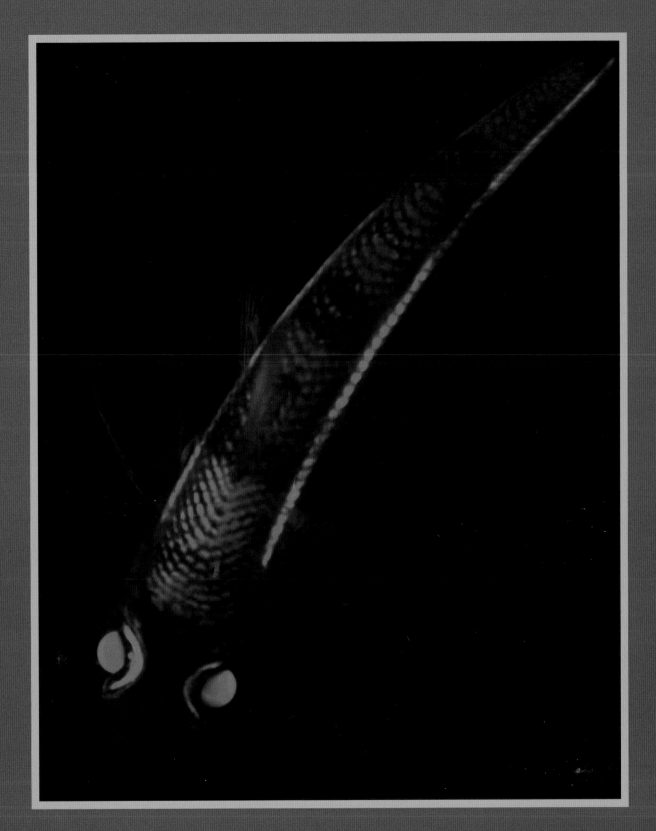
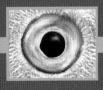
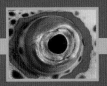

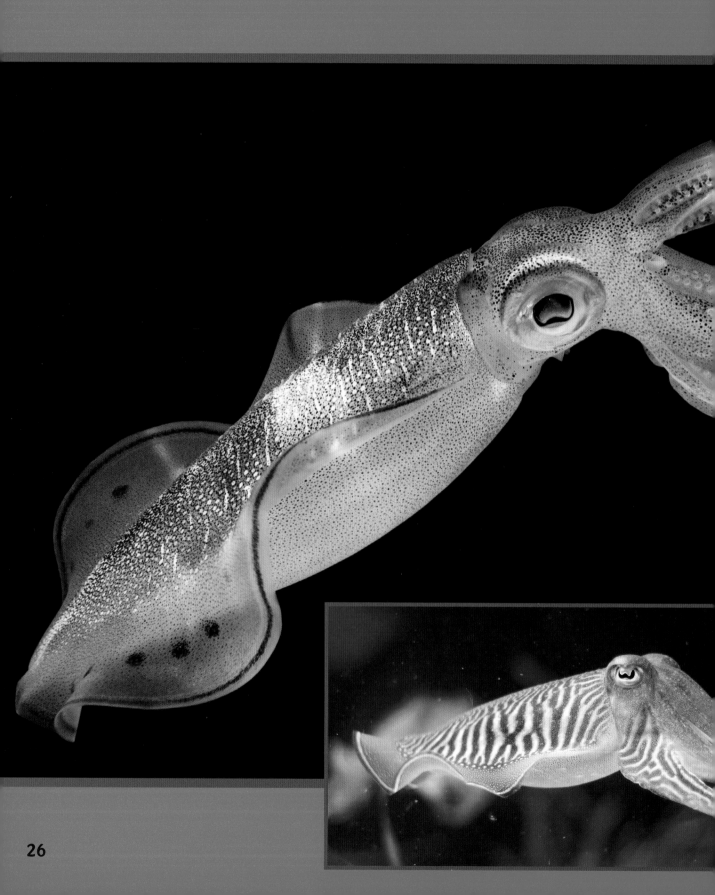

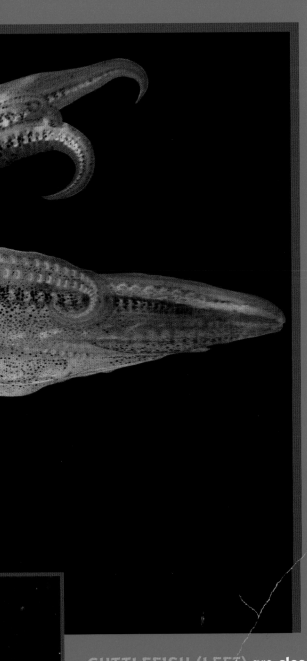

SQUID EYES

The colossal squid has the largest eye of any animal on earth. Scientists who measured one of the eyes said it was bigger than a Frisbee!

No one knows for sure why squid have such large eyes, but it may help them hunt in three dimensions — above, beside, and below. It may also help them escape from predators such as fast-swimming whales.

TECH TALK: Squid have a type of vision called binocular vision, just like people have. Each of their two eyes sees the area nearby from a slightly different angle, but the images overlap in the middle and combine so they only "see" one image.

CUTTLEFISH (LEFT) are close relatives of squid and octopusses and live in deep ocean waters. Cuttlefish are able to change their skin colors and patterns very fast to hide from predators. Like most squid and octopusses, though, cuttlefish are color blind so they can't see their own bright colors!

CHECK IT OUT: Take a close look at the cool "W" shape of this cuttlefish's eye. The "W" shape may work like a pair of sunglasses, blocking the glare of sunlight coming through the water from the surface.

CRAB EYES

A nimals such as lobsters, shrimp, and crabs have compound eyes. Each compound eye is made of many lenses, and is found on the tip of an eyestalk. Insects and spiders also have compound eyes, but they do not have eyestalks. To learn more about compound eyes, turn the page.

Not all types (species) of crabs have the same types of eyestalks. Some crab eyes are on tall eyestalks and some are on short eyestalks, close to their bodies. Their eyestalks can move in many directions, so these animals can see in many directions without ever moving their heads!

CHECK IT OUT! Scientists have found that crabs that live on rocky beaches have rounder eyes that are farther apart, while the eyes of crabs that live on flat beaches are usually taller and closer together. Look at the eyes on the crabs on the left-hand page. Are they all the same? What type of beach do you think these crabs live on, rocky or flat?

SNAILS HAVE EYESTALKS, TOO! For animals such as land snails, which are low to the ground and can't move fast, having eyes on top of their heads can help them find more food and avoid predators. These snails can even raise their eyestalks up and down when they want to see higher or lower! Cool trick, huh?

FLY EYES

A fly's eyes are very different from your eyes. Instead of two single eyes, flies have thousands of small lenses (called facets) that work together in each compound eye. In most flies, the eye areas bulge outward on the sides of their heads, which lets more lenses fit in the eye area.

If you want to look to the left or to the right, or up or down, you can move just your eyes or just your head — or you can move both your eyes and your head. Flies have a hard, outer surface on their bodies, called an exoskeleton, which does not allow their heads to move well. Also, flies don't have muscles to move their eyes, like people do, so a fly has to turn its entire body to see in a new direction.

Like most animals with compound eyes, flies cannot see very far. If every desk in your classroom had a fly sitting on it, none of them would be able to see your teacher standing in the front of the room. Animals with compound eyes can see a lot of detail close up, though, the way you can see detail through a magnifying glass or a microscope. Compound eyes are also good for seeing objects that are moving, such as flying bugs and predators.

TOTALLY COOL:
If you look at a dragonfly (right) or a housefly (left), it's easy to see the animal's two large compound eyes. But did you know dragonflies, like many other flying insects, actually have FIVE eyes — two large compound eyes and three simple eyes? Scientists think these three extra eyes help the animals fly at the correct height so they don't crash into the ground.

Guess Who!

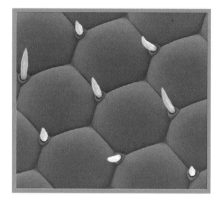

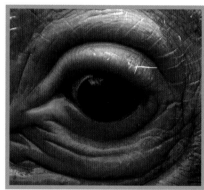

? ? ?

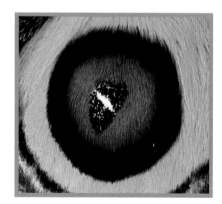

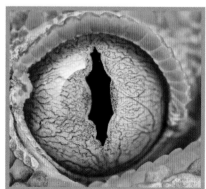

TURN PAGE TO FIND OUT . . . TURN PAGE TO FIND OUT . . . TURN PAGE TO FIND OUT . . .

Guess Who!

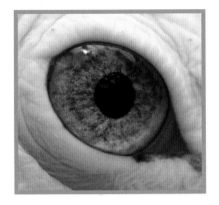

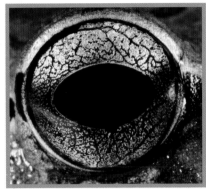

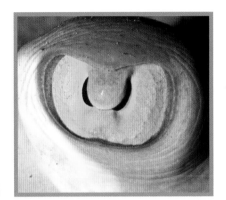

?   ?   ?

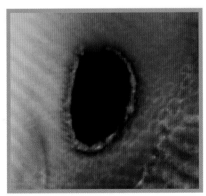

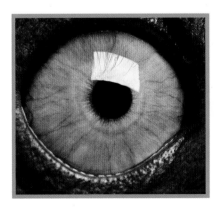

TURN PAGE TO FIND OUT . . . TURN PAGE TO FIND OUT . . . TURN PAGE TO FIND OUT . . .

Guess Who!

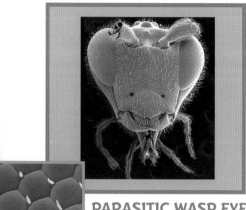

PARASITIC WASP EYE
(Under scanning electron microscope)

HIPPOPO EYE

GOAT EYE

MOTH EYESPOTS
(Fake eyes that fool predators)

GECKO EYE

SPIDER EYE

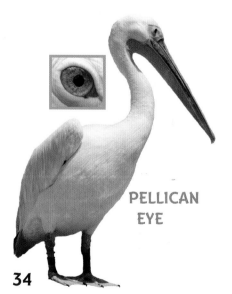

PELLICAN EYE

FROG EYE

STINGRAY EYE

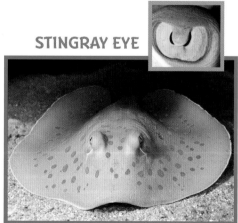

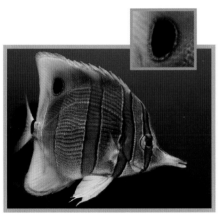

SUGAR GLIDER EYE

Glossary

BINOCULAR VISION: The ability to see one image from two eyes at the same time. The brain combines the images from each eye into one, single image. Animals such as rabbits, birds, and horses that have one eye on each side of their head, see two different images. This type of vision is called **monocular vision.**

COMPOUND EYES: This type of eye is found in a large group (phylum) of animals called the arthropods, including insects, spiders, crabs, and lobsters. Compound eyes use facets to collect visual information. Some compound eyes have just a few facets, while others have thousands of facets. Compound eyes are very good at seeing motion.

EYESPOTS: Patterns on an animal, often far away from its eyes, that look like eyes and confuse predators. Eyespots are often seen in caterpillars, adult butterflies and moths, and fish.

EYESTALKS: A thin protrusion found on the tops of the heads of crabs, lobsters, and snails. The eye is found on the tip of the eyestalk, and animals can move their eyestalks in different directions, helping them see better.

NICTITATING MEMBRANE: Also called the "third eyelid," this thin, see-through membrane is found on the eyes of reptiles, birds, and sharks. It serves as a protective layer. Some mammals, such as polar bears and seals, also have nictitating membranes.

NOCTURNAL: Active at night. Most animals that are nocturnal have adaptations that help their eyes work better in low light.

PREDATOR: An animal that hunts other animals to eat. The animals that predators hunt are called prey.

SIMPLE EYES: Eyes that have only one lens. Human eyes have just one lens, so we have simple eyes.

TAPETUM: A layer of tissue found in many night-hunting animals that reflects light, helping the animals to see better.

BUTTERFLY FISH EYESPOT

CROWNED SIFAKA LEMUR EYE

How Our Eyes Work . . .

Human eyes have several parts to them, and each part does something important. The **pupil** is the black circle in the middle of your eye and the place where light enters the eye. The colored area around the pupil is the **iris.** In people, the **iris** can be brown, blue, green, or hazel. The **iris** is a muscle that can pull the **pupil** open wider to let more light into the eye. The **cornea** is the clear coating over our entire outer eye. Have you ever had something go in your eye that made it all red and watery for the rest of the day? If so, you may have scratched your **cornea**.

The **lens** is right behind the **iris.** Its job is to focus a picture on your **retina.** The **retina** is the inside back of the eye. The **retina** has more than 120 million cells called **photoreceptors** that gather information about shapes, colors, and details. This information is sent to the **brain** for processing. The **brain** combines the information from both eyes into one image, and then you **see!**

Index

The End!

ACKNOWLEDGMENTS

Research by the following biologists and institutions contributed many of the fascinating facts in this book: Richard Berry, (Australian National University), Curt Deckert, Russell D. Hamer, Kelsie Jackson, Michael F. Land, Ken and Catherine Lohmann, Desmond Morris, Dan-Eric Nilsson, G. Nalbach, H.O. Nalbach, Eric Warrant, James Wood, and J. Zeil, Duke University Primate Center, Museum of Vision, and the Florida Museum of Natural History.

PHOTO CREDITS

Pages 32 and 34, top left, Dr. Robert Wharton, Texas A&M University; image created at the Digital Microscopy Facility, Mount Allison University (www.mta.ca/dmf).